Career Planning
for Tweens

Essential Skills for Career Exploration and
Development, Helping Preteens Discover
Their Passion and Find Their Dream Job

Isabella Wells

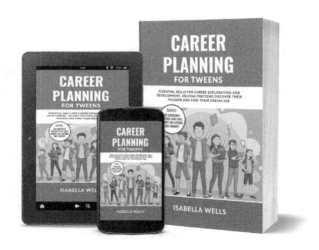

As a career counselor specializing in guiding tweens through the exciting journey of career planning, I've crafted this book to empower young readers with the knowledge, tools, and resources they need to navigate the ever-changing landscape of the job market. Each chapter is designed to spark curiosity, inspire exploration, and cultivate confidence as tweens embark on the path to discovering their passions and shaping their future careers. Let's embark on this adventure together and unlock the possibilities that lie ahead!

Isabella Wells

Contents

Introduction   7

Chapter One   11

Understanding Your Capabilities and Hobbies   11

    Discovering What You are Good at and Love Doing   11

    Taking Personality and Aptitude Assessments   13

    Career Exploration Activities and Games   16

Chapter Two   19

Popular Career Fields   19

    Creative Careers (Art, Design, Performing Arts)   19

    Helping Careers (Teaching, Medicine, Social Work)   22

    Technology and Science Careers   26

Chapter Three   31

Goal Setting for Tweens   31

Writing SMART Goals   31

Creating a Vision Board   34

Tracking Progress and Milestones   37

Chapter Four   **41**

School Subjects That Matter   **41**

Core Classes (Math, Science, English, History) 41

Electives and Extracurriculars   44

Developing Good Study Habits   48

Chapter Five   **53**

Essential Skills to Develop   **53**

Communication and Public Speaking   53

Time Management and Organization   57

Problem-Solving and Teamwork   61

Chapter Six   **67**

Earning and Managing Money   **67**

Budgeting and Saving for Goals   67

Tween Entrepreneurship Ideas   70

Introduction to Banking   73

Chapter Seven   **77**

Work-Life Balance   77

   Exploring Hobbies and Passions   77

   Managing Stress and Overwhelm   80

   Importance of Family and Friends   83

Chapter Eight   87

Getting Experience   87

   Volunteering Opportunities   87

   Job Shadowing a Professional   91

   Attending Career Fairs and Events   94

Chapter Nine   99

Believing in Yourself   99

   Building Confidence   99

   Overcoming Fears and Doubts   103

   Finding Role Models and Mentors   106

Chapter Ten   111

Involving Family   111

   Having Career Conversations   111

   Setting Expectations with Parents   114

   Making a Career Plan Together   117

Exclusive Bonus   **121**

30 emerging career that will shape the future
job market   121

Introduction

Dear Ambitious Tween,

Can you feel it? That spark of curiosity and excitement stirring inside you as you glimpse the incredible world of possibilities awaiting? The thrill of pondering all the amazing paths your future could take, each one beaming with potential for adventure, challenge, and personal fulfillment?

If you're reading these words, it means you've already awakened to the realization that your journey is yours to shape. That despite your youth, the power to craft an extraordinary life is pulsing within you, ready to be unleashed through bold exploration and unwavering determination.

This book, Career Planning for Tweens, is your official launch pad into a mind-expanding voyage of self-discovery, audacious dream-chasing, and future-crafting. Within these pages, you'll unearth strategies for pinpointing your innate talents, connecting them to careers that energize your passions, and mapping out an actionable roadmap toward realizing your grandest ambitions.

Brace yourself to be exposed to an astounding breadth of captivating professions you've likely never imagined – careers at the bleeding edge of technological frontiers, careers advancing global sustainability, careers channeling creativity into impactful entertainment and art. The world eagerly awaits those who will transform it through innovation, compassion, and vision.

More than just exploring potential occupations, you're about to embark on a powerful journey of self-discovery. Through thought-provoking exercises and self-assessments, you'll unlock unprecedented insights into your unique strengths, motivations, and the environments where you'll positively thrive. Preparing your mindset is paramount for resilience amidst life's inevitable challenges.

Although the gravity of shaping your future may feel daunting at times, you'll never navigate these uncharted terrains alone. This book becomes your trusted co-pilot and guide, answering your boldest questions and equipping you with time-tested wisdom for achieving career success. Mentors, role models, and encouraging voices will inspire you from the sidelines at every step.

In these transformative years between childhood and the cusp of adulthood, you possess unparalleled power to intentionally design the life of your dreams rather than stumble into chances. The exploratory pathways illuminated in this book provide clarity amidst ambiguity – allowing you to sledgehammer through fears and harness your spirited ambition.

So embrace your curiosity, tween trailblazer, and let it steer you into this whirlwind of self-exploration and career world-building. Let the kaleidoscope of human potential expand before your very eyes! Having the courage to be boldly introspective at this pivotal inflection point is the first step towards manifesting the extraordinary future awaiting you.

Now, take a deep breath and get ready to embark on the single most empowering journey of your lifetime so far. Your brilliant future, crafted in your image, is finally ready to be launched!

Chapter One

Understanding Your Capabilities and Hobbies

Discovering What You are Good at and Love Doing

When you are a tween, you are in the thrilling process of coming into your own and finding out what makes you happy. Before delving into possible job routes, it is important to take stock of your strengths and interests.

A talent is an innate skill that one can perform well without deliberate practice. A skill could be anything from an aptitude for music, acting, or sketching to a prowess in the written word, computer technology, or mathematics. Conversely, what I mean by "passions" are things that truly excite and motivate me.

One technique to identify your skills is to think back on activities you've particularly enjoyed or succeeded at in school, extracurriculars, or hobbies. Tell me something easy that made you proud. Another way is to ask friends, family members, or teachers what strengths they've noticed in you.

Hobbies like photography, gaming, cooking, and athletics may inspire you to pursue your passions. Or it could be intellectual disciplines that excite your curiosity like marine biology, coding, or ancient civilizations. Reflect on the topics you find yourself researching or talking about the most.

It's crucial to note that your talents and hobbies can be extremely broad at this age and may evolve. The secret is to maintain an open mind. The idea isn't to pick one specific job route yet, but rather to start investigating general topics that drive and invigorate you.

Grab a notebook and write notes of all the talents and passions you can identify about yourself so far. Don't filter or criticize the lists – simply jot down whatever comes to mind. This self-reflection can provide valuable perspective as you begin examining prospective job possibilities.

Taking Personality and Aptitude Assessments

While self-reflection is vital, personality and aptitude evaluations can provide much deeper insights into what makes you distinctive. These tools are designed to scientifically measure your natural tendencies, abilities, values, and motivators.

Personality evaluations analyze characteristics of your character and behavior including whether you're more introverted or extroverted, logical or creative, detail-oriented or big-picture-minded. Some examples are the Myers-Briggs Type Indicator and the DISC evaluation.

The results shed light on appropriate work environments and cultures, communication methods, and paths that could be invigorating versus exhausting for your personality type. You may learn you flourish in collaborative team environments or prefer more independent tasks for example.

Aptitude exams, on the other hand, examine your abilities and potential in specific skill areas like verbal, numerical, mechanical, spatial, and clerical talents. The ASVAB (Armed Services Vocational Aptitude Battery) is one extensively utilized multiple-aptitude test battery.

By identifying the qualities you have an inherent propensity for, you may start matching those talents to professional fields that employ those skills. Perhaps you'll find you have excellent numerical talents appropriate for accounting, or great spatial skills for architectural or design professions.

Many schools give access to personality and aptitude testing, or you can find some credible versions online (be careful to gain parental approval first). As you analyze your results, make notes on professions or industries that seem to meet your preferences and abilities.

Don't get too hung up if your assessment results disagree with your current interests – these are the only tools to bring further self-awareness as you traverse this trip. Trust your gut when a course feels genuinely exhilarating to you.

Career Exploration Activities and Games

Once you have a rough feel of your talents, interests, and personality traits, it's time for the fun part — researching numerous job choices! There are many intriguing activities and games meant to expose you to diverse jobs.

One wonderful approach is taking a career assessment quiz or survey. These interactive tools ask about your favorite school subjects, talents, interests, and employment preferences. Based on your comments, you'll receive recommended career matches with descriptions and multi-media job previews to check out.

The Bureau of Labor Statistics and Occupational Outlook Handbook websites contain fantastic free career exploration resources. Or check out quiz apps and websites like Open Colleges Career Quiz or the Princeton Review Careers After COVID-19 Quiz.

Another hands-on way to explore is through employment simulation games and movies. These provide a fascinating insight into "a day in the life" of different vocations. For example, you may get to virtually experience being a pilot and flying an airplane, or strolling through the activities of a video game designer, forensic scientist, or chef.

Games like Rounds: Franklin Rapper Career Explorer and Mission Biotech tap on preteen interests while exposing you to other fields. Or let your imagination soar with open-ended sandbox-style games where you can take on different positions and construct your professional adventures.

Lastly, don't forget about classic approaches like attending career fairs or setting up job shadowing experiences. These allow chances to interact one-on-one with professionals, ask questions, and witness them in action. Your school may offer these possibilities or you might explore community activities.

The key is pursuing things that allow you to have pleasure while exploring new potential avenues. Approach this approach with an adventurous spirit of curiosity and possibilities. You never know what career can grab your interest next!

Chapter Two

Popular Career Fields

Creative Careers (Art, Design, Performing Arts)

Do you live for opportunities to express yourself through artistic outlets? Do you find yourself continually sketching, composing novels, or choreographing dance moves? If so, you may be destined for a fulfilling creative career!

The creative industries comprise a wide range of intriguing professions based upon innovative self-expression and bringing visionary ideas to reality. Let's explore some of the most popular paths:

Fine Arts & Crafts

For tweens with a passion for painting, sculpting, photography, or handcrafted arts, careers like artist, illustrator, art instructor, museum curator, or art director could be fulfilling professions. These visually-minded creatives generate meaningful works to inspire, embellish environments, or contribute to commercial and media ventures.

Performing Arts

Born performers may gravitate towards occupations like actor, dancer, singer, musician, or multimedia performance. Can you picture yourself mesmerizing audiences on stage, in films, or recording vivid voices in the studio? Performers use their talents to educate, encourage, and bring stories and emotions to life.

Writing & Publishing

Wordsmith tweens who are excellent storytellers or exceptional writers could find their calling as novelists, playwrights, screenwriters, journalists, editors, or copywriters. Careers in publishing allow you to generate impactful narratives, thought-provoking content, or engaging commercial messaging.

Design

Those with great visual and aesthetic ability may be lured to design-centric occupations such as graphic designer, multimedia artist, animator, fashion designer, interior designer, or architect. Designers integrate technological talents with artistic vision to make appealing digital graphics, clothes, living environments, goods, and more.

Culinary Arts

For the culinary masterminds continuously experimenting with new flavors, becoming a chef, baker, food critic or restaurateur could be your tasty destiny! These occupations enable you to pour creativity into crafting scrumptious dishes and creative dining experiences.

No matter which creative path speaks to you, these occupations reward inventiveness, personal expression, and pushing the boundaries of what's possible. You'll spend your days developing your artistic talents while offering something unique and meaningful to the world.

However, it's crucial to realize that many creative occupations can be very competitive with intermittent income streams, especially when first starting. Developing entrepreneurial skills, tenacity and numerous income streams is crucial. But for the properly driven preteen with natural skill and enthusiasm, the rewards are huge!

Helping Careers (Teaching, Medicine, Social Work)

At your core, are you someone who enjoys being of service to others and wants to make a positive difference? If the notion of caring, protecting, or inspiring people energizes you, choosing a helping career could be an awesome fit.

While challenging, these careers bring unmatched fulfillment from influencing lives in meaningful ways each day. Some top assisting fields attracting dedicated tweens include:

Education

Teachers quite literally shape the future by passing on knowledge to kids. As an educator, you could select to deal with specific age groups like elementary, middle, or high school. Or become a specialist teacher for disciplines like art, music, gym, or special education. The mission? Igniting a passion for learning while helping kids attain their potential!

Healthcare

With roles like doctor, nurse, physician assistant, dentist, or veterinarian, you'd have the capacity to treat and promote the health of people or animals. Tweens interested in science and medicine could find meaning in diagnosing and treating injuries or disorders, delivering top-notch professional care, or even discovering new treatments and cures.

Counseling & Mental Health

Therapists, psychologists, social workers, and counselors help people overcome great personal problems, trauma, and obstacles to enhance their mental health and live satisfying lives. You could choose to specialize in areas like marriage/family, bereavement, addictions, or child/adolescent counseling.

Community & Social Service

If you have a heart for philanthropy, civil service, or advocacy, professions like non-profit director, social worker, community organizer, or politician allow you to protect vulnerable populations, run programs for the underprivileged, implement meaningful policies and initiatives, or raise awareness around critical causes.

While courses of study and certifications differ, most assisting occupations emphasize strong interpersonal skills for engaging with the individuals you'll serve. You'll also require caring instincts, empathy, resilience, and a deep amount of patience.

The ability to personally enhance people's lives is invaluable - whether that's by teaching and mentoring, offering competent care and treatment, counseling guidance, or safeguarding human rights and resources. If your motivation comes from serving others, these vocations deliver that pleasant fulfillment daily.

Technology and Science Careers

Our world is continuously evolving because of innovative advancements in scientific research, engineering, computer technology, and more. Does digging into how things function and applying reasoning to tackle complex challenges thrill you? A future in tech or sciences could be a calling.

These areas offer boundless chances for the eternally curious tween who yearns to ask questions, conduct experiments, analyze data, and seek answers to real-world problems. Let's investigate some possibilities:

Computer Technology
If you're the child who's always fiddling with code or consuming the latest software and app news, positions like computer programmer, web

developer, software engineer, systems analyst, or even ethical hacker could be your niche. These technological experts construct the digital tools, platforms, and systems that enable our modern world.

Engineering problem-solvers may be lured to engineering occupations where you'll produce creative goods, buildings, machines, or systems. Some engineering branches to consider are mechanical, electrical, civil, aerospace, biomedical, chemical, or computer hardware. You'll apply science and math ideas to develop safe, efficient, and cutting-edge designs.

Research & Sciences

Scientific researchers, chemists, biologists, physicists, mathematicians, environmental scientists, and archeologists regularly generate discoveries that improve human knowledge and understanding. You could dive into topics like medicine, genetics, ecology, oceanography, astrophysics, and more, unearthing insights about our world.

Data & Mathematics

Our data-driven era gives us exceptional prospects for statisticians, data analysts, data scientists, and mathematicians. These individuals collect, analyze, and discover meaning in complicated data sets to identify patterns or build data-based solutions for corporations, organizations, and researchers in practically any area.

Emerging Technologies

Trailblazers with great goals may seek to pioneer the next technology frontier in domains like artificial intelligence, robots, virtual/augmented reality, blockchain, cybersecurity, and more. These continually expanding areas need youthful, imaginative minds to keep pushing boundaries and creating our future potential.

What unifies all these approaches is a foundation of curiosity, analytical thinking, and continually attempting to apply logic and facts to comprehend or create something novel. With a natural propensity for sciences and math, plus hefty doses of imagination and perseverance, these vocations empower you to keep expanding what's possible.

Chapter Three

Goal Setting for Tweens

Writing SMART Goals

They say a goal without a plan is simply a wish. That's why understanding how to make effective objectives is such an important ability, especially for driven tweens anxious to start working towards their hopes and ambitions. One powerful method is using the SMART goal framework:

Specific

Vague goals like "get better at math" or "explore careers" aren't very motivating or actionable. You need laser-focused specificity to target what you genuinely want to achieve. Practice reframing goals into concrete words like "Earn an A in Algebra this semester" or "Job shadow two professionals in healthcare fields by June."

Measurable

Measurable goals solve the soul-crushing issue of "How will I know when I've succeeded?" By connecting quantifiable measurements, you create crystal clear finish lines to aspire for. For example: Read 25 books from the suggested career reading list. Score a 90% or above on the career aptitude test. Submit 3 applications for summer internships.

Achievable

While objectives should stretch you, they can't be utter pipe dreams with no prospect of reaching them. Achievable suggests the objective is possible, but will require true commitment, guts, and putting in the work to make it happen. A feasible aim for a tween may be winning a regional speech competition versus becoming President...at least for now!

Relevant

Relevancy ensures your goals are worth the effort by aligning with greater life reasons or aspirations that matter to you right now. A relevant objective connects back to your basic values, and talents and explores possibilities you're passionate about. For school-aged tweens, most goals should emphasize skill development, self-discovery, and future preparation.

Time-bound

Attaching a clear deadline creates very important motivation and urgency. A goal's timescale could be next week, 3 months from now, or before high school starts. Just make sure it's reasonable enough to focus your efforts, but not too distant that it loses its appealing drive. Time-bound goals generate observable progress you can be inspired by.

Let's put it into practice: "Submit 3 job shadowing applications at companies I'm interested in by August 1st." This goal is specific to job shadowing, measurable with 3 completed applications, achievable based on time/resources available, relevant to exploring interests, and time-bound to the August 1st due date.

Having this level of detail removes any ambiguity and transforms goals from wishful thinking into deliberate marching orders. Start utilizing the SMART methodology when defining goals around academics, extracurriculars, career readiness, and any other areas of focus. Having SMART goals gives you a clear plan for investing your everyday efforts.

Creating a Vision Board

We all need physical reminders of what we're striving for to keep our motivation strong. That's where vision boards may be a powerful tool for tweens aiming to attain goals and visualize their desires for the future.

At its foundation, a vision board is a collage of images, photographs, and affirmations that reflect whatever you wish to make actual in your life. It's a fascinating practice for planting those desires into your subconscious mind and keeping inspiration.

Creating a vision board may be a fun arts & crafts project to let your creativity show! Gather magazines, print-outs of motivational quotes, colored sheets, scissors, glue or tape, and a poster board. The magic happens as you methodically cut out words and visuals that relate to your aims or the feelings you desire to experience.

When designing your board, try for a balance of images linked to your job objectives, academic dreams, attributes you aspire to develop, skills to learn, experiences to manifest, and your overall mentality for success. Don't limit yourself to only career - include representations for all facets of the life you want.

For example, you could include pictures of your favorite school subjects, a university you'd love to attend, job titles or professions that ignite your passion, powerful words like "resilience" or "courage", hobbies you wish to take up like photography, or cut-outs depicting your desired income, home, travel adventures or positive social circle.

Once your photographs are organized in a visually attractive fashion, hang your vision board in a space where you'll see it every day as a motivating reminder of all the amazing things you're striving to co-create in your life. Let it encourage you to take action towards your SMART goals.

You may even make vision board exercises a group activity with friends or classmates - sharing your boards and supporting one other's adventures. For tweens, vision boards inspire big-goal thinking while merging creativity and art.

Tracking Progress and Milestones

Chasing huge objectives and ambitious dreams is immensely fulfilling yet can often be discouraging when you feel stuck or aren't seeing progress as soon as desired. That's why actively tracking your goal-pursuit process is so crucial to sustaining motivation and perseverance.

The simple act of monitoring and recording how far you've come provides accountability while allowing you to appreciate every milestone and win along the way, no matter how minor. Those tiny victories compound over time into huge growth!

There are numerous innovative ways tweens can track objectives and recognize achievements:

Journey Maps

These linear representations help you to sketch out the incremental actions required to proceed towards your greater objectives. Journey maps can feature encouraging phrases, graphics emblematic of key milestones, and places to note triumphs or lessons gained after completing each stage.

Habit Trackers

Dream careers frequently entail adopting new habits and practices. Habit trackers are checklists or calendars where you may tick off each day that you perform your chosen habits, like studying for an hour, networking, or any consistent routine you're attempting to instill.

Accomplishment Lists or Visual Trackers

For celebrating triumphs, develop a running list, vision board section, or visual tracker to document each accomplishment, no matter how tiny. Continually watching your triumphs mount up fuels self-confidence and delight surrounding your development.

Job/Activity Logs

Journaling your experiences might help extract essential insights while monitoring personal improvement. Keep a notebook noting tasks worked on, skills practiced, research notes, interviews or job shadows attended and any hurdles conquered along the route. These logs also become resume-building materials!

Project Dashboards

Tweens managing larger projects or balancing various goals could use a dashboard for tracking all active workstreams, deliverables, open tasks, or blocks visualized in one commanding perspective. Checking tasks off the list feels very fulfilling.

Whatever tracking systems you pick, be sure to add celebrations and prizes for achievements. Incentives make the trip fun and reaffirm your commitment to making steady strides every day.

Consider sharing progress updates with parents, instructors, or mentors supporting your pathway.

Consistent recording of your dreams and accomplishments will provide you with a confidence-building vantage point on how much you've advanced. Staying focused on achieving incremental progress eventually leads to spectacular achievements over time!

Chapter Four

School Subjects That Matter

Core Classes (Math, Science, English, History)

While pursuing vocational interests and developing your talents outside the classroom is crucial, your achievement in core academic courses sets the essential basis for future success. Math, science, English, and history may not seem immediately linked to your chosen job, but succeeding in these disciplines promotes critical thinking, analytical, and communication abilities that will help you in practically any profession.

Mathematics

From crunching numbers to evaluating data, math principles, and quantitative reasoning abilities are highly sought across numerous professions. Taking classes like algebra, geometry, statistics, and calculus exercises your problem-solving ability while helping you to think rationally and precisely. Careers in finance, engineering, computer science, research, and business necessitate good math ability.

Science

Understanding science isn't just crucial for jobs in healthcare, technology, or environmental disciplines. The scientific technique of formulating hypotheses, performing experiments, and drawing evidence-based conclusions provides vital critical thinking skills applicable to any field. Biology, chemistry, physics, and earth/space science classes increase your scientific literacy and capacity to address difficulties systematically.

English Language Arts

Effective written and verbal communication is crucial no matter what route you take. Literature, reading comprehension, vocabulary growth, grammar, and composition classes increase your ability to understand texts, construct strong arguments, and express yourself clearly. You'll also explore creativity through poetry, fiction, and non-fiction writing. These skills are crucial for presentations, cooperation, and workplace success.

History/Social Studies

While studying historical events and civilizations may seem irrelevant, history cultivates an understanding of numerous cultures, geographies, and political and economic systems shaping our present world. Learning to study sources, assess numerous perspectives, and comprehend the big-picture context behind wars or societal upheavals improves critical thinking and global citizenship - skills for any vocation.

Rather than looking at these courses as required duties, consider them as opportunities to learn universal qualities that will open doors. Math teaches logical reasoning. Science develops curiosity and intellectual humility. Reading and writing enhance clear communication and creative expression. History gives context for understanding complex human experiences.

Consistently pushing oneself to succeed at a high level in these fundamental areas communicates your work ethic, dedication, and commitment to self-improvement - very desirable attributes to potential employers, admissions officials, and mentors. So stay focused, ask questions, study diligently, and watch as larger fields of possibilities develop.

Electives and Extracurriculars

While the core curriculum provides a firm academic background, elective programs, and extracurricular activities allow you to creatively explore particular interests and find latent abilities. These are essential possibilities for well-rounded development that can favorably affect your career trajectory.

Electives

Most schools provide a varied choice of elective or specialty disciplines like art, music, drama, film studies, computer programming, woodshop, culinary arts, foreign languages, journalism, and more. Don't be hesitant to explore with electives outside of your usual comfort zone! You may surprise and unearth a new passion that could blossom into a satisfying vocation.

For the tech-savvy tween, electives like coding, 3D design, or multimedia production could introduce you to in-demand skills in profitable careers like software development, animation, or video game creation. Taking drafting, architectural, or engineering classes could inspire curiosity about building and manufacturing employment. Those with creativity may find self-expression through art, dance, music, or drama electives that open horizons in entertainment and creative services.

Not only do electives allow you to sample diverse subjects, but specializing and upgrading your curriculum shows universities and future employers outstanding commitment. Building targeted knowledge and portfolios provides you with a competitive edge.

Extracurriculars

Extracurricular clubs and activities provide hands-on ways to build important soft skills sought in any field. Joining theatre, debate, or DECA (marketing) organizations increases public speaking talents. Student government builds leadership experience. Environmental or community service clubs foster teamwork and social responsibility.

If athletics is your passion, joining school sports develops collaboration, dedication, and prolonged hard work - skills appreciated across practically every career sector. Those interested in healthcare careers might join health occupation organizations like HOSA to start investigating the field. Technology enthusiasts obtain coding and hardware experience through robotics teams or computer clubs.

Additionally, extracurriculars provide networking opportunities and ways to start creating your brand. Consistent involvement demonstrates commitment and well-roundedness to admissions officers and possible employers.

So use your school's electives and activities as channels for self-discovery! When you find courses or hobbies you enjoy, delve further by seeking advanced classes, competitions, or applying for leadership roles. Thoughtful engagement gives you richer experiences to discuss during interviews and puts you one step closer to establishing your chosen job path.

Developing Good Study Habits

No matter how enthusiastic you are about a subject, mastering good study methods and routines is vital for absorbing information and retaining knowledge. Developing strong study habits today will pay dividends for academic achievement and future career success.

Here are some crucial behaviors to cultivate:

Create a Designated Study Space

An orderly, peaceful, distraction-free study environment like a desk area or reading nook indicates to your brain it's time to focus. Gather things like pencils, paper, and calculators within reach so you don't have to keep getting up. Personalizing your space with inspirational photos might help motivate you.

Follow the Pomodoro Time Management Method
Work in 25-minute intense bursts, followed by 5-minute rests to refuel. The Pomodoro approach minimizes burnout and procrastination by introducing restorative pauses into your productivity. Time-tracking tools can assist with implementing this cycle.

Take Effective Notes
Go beyond simply copying information by selecting significant subjects, summarizing main concepts, and asking thoughtful questions in your notes to truly interact with the material. The Cornell Note system helps increase comprehension.

Space Out Study Sessions

Spacing out many study sessions for the same content over several days is demonstrated to boost recollection versus marathon cram sessions. Start reviewing content as soon as it's been covered in class.

Teach Concepts Back to Build Mastery

The easiest approach to solidify your knowledge is by expressing concepts out loud or attempting to teach someone else. Verbalizing your understanding fortifies neuronal networks.

Stay Active

Moving around actively activates your brain to increase focus and information absorption. Look for opportunities to review notes while stretching or pacing about. Exercise before significant tests can help increase memory and cognitive ability.

Reward Progress

Celebrating minor triumphs through favorite snacks, hobbies, or breaks keeps you engaged and invested in the process. Set checkpoints for treating yourself upon hitting critical goals.

Get Enough Sleep and Nutrition
Your attention depletes quickly without enough sleep and fuelling your body with nutritious foods. Prioritize at least 8 hours of relaxation and keep consistency with study sessions following nutritious breakfasts and lunches.

By proactively building strong study routines and habits today, you're setting the scene for sustained academic performance that will carry you through higher education and into your future professional objectives.

Chapter Five

Essential Skills to Develop

Communication and Public Speaking

Effective communication is probably one of the most crucial abilities for success in any career field. After all, how can you share your creative ideas, deliver instructions, or inspire others without the ability to articulate yourself effectively and confidently? Start strengthening your communication prowess today and you'll have a big competitive edge.

Interpersonal Communication

Beyond merely speaking and writing ability, excellent interpersonal skills are crucial for productive job interactions. Practice active listening by allowing people to talk without interrupting them, then rephrase crucial points to confirm knowledge. Learn to appropriately change your communication approach to diverse audiences. Reading social cues like body language and tone promotes empathy.

For challenging conversations, emotional intelligence coaching can help you reply calmly rather than with negativity. Respectfully stating your views while validating others' viewpoints is a superpower. Master polite eye contact, solid handshakes, and remembering names/details about others. These qualities generate trust and better partnerships.

Public Speaking

Does the prospect of public speaking make your palms sweat? Don't worry - glossophobia (the fear of public speaking) is highly prevalent, but also entirely conquerable with practice and the appropriate approaches.

Make friends with anxiety management strategies like power posing, deep breathing, positive self-talk, and overlearning/memorizing your information. Join your school's debating club or theatrical department to receive maximum stage time. Toastmasters groups also provide a helpful atmosphere for developing speaking ability.

When presenting speeches or presentations, focus on speaking deliberately and projecting your voice confidently. Incorporating comedy, analogies, personal tales, and rhetorical strategies like rhetorical questions keeps your audience captivated. Use lively hand motions and movement to radiate energy. Visual aids are crucial too - utilize slide decks, props, audio/video clips, and activities to support your messages.

Most essential, don't just present - seek to have a true dialogue that addresses your audience's specific wants, pain areas, and objections. Welcome Q&A to display active listening and thoughtfully validate people's remarks.

Written Communication

Today's professionals must be outstanding writers proficient at creating concise emails, reports, proposals, messages, and more for varied stakeholders. Study good writing structure with effective hooks, thesis statements, supporting evidence, and captivating conclusions.

Pay great attention to grammar, spelling, tone, and word choice. Writing succinctly and avoiding too complicated terminology promotes readability. Back up crucial claims through convincing storytelling and appropriate examples. Then proofread ruthlessly, ensuring no errors.

Most importantly, learn to modify your writing style adequately for the communication format and audience, whether formal or informal. Refine editing abilities to provide constructive feedback to others on their written work.

Start a blog or video channel to exhibit your communication talents while creating an early personal brand online. Leverage tools like Grammarly, which delivers real-time writing critique. With continual practice, your communication abilities will flourish.

Time Management and Organization

In our fast-paced, demanding world, mastering time management and organizing skills allows you to utilize your most precious resource — your time and energy – wisely. Adopting tactics for enhancing productivity early will pay advantages for managing competing priorities throughout your career.

Time Management Techniques

Ever feel like there's simply never enough time in the day to get it all done? Implementing time management frameworks like the Pomodoro Technique (working in focused 25-minute sprints), eating that frog (tackling the biggest, most critical chores first), or timeboxing where you assign specific periods for activities, can maximize your daily production.

Prioritizing and avoiding distractions/procrastination is key. Make a habit of constantly updating to-do lists to track your most essential deliverables. Plot up specific work blocks on your calendar each week. Single-tasking (focused on one task until completion) is more efficient than multitasking.

Organization Habits

Does your backpack, locker, or office feel like a never-ending swirl of mess and clutter? Disorganization decreases motivation and makes things take longer to find. Conversely, being consciously ordered brings peace of mind and efficiency.

Develop systems for storing digital files/notes in clearly designated folders available anytime. Dedicate physical places for supplies and papers, keeping them frequently. Keep a neat calendar or planner for noting due dates, appointments, and obligations. Design checklists to ensure you complete essential sequences correctly each time.

At school, maintain a strategic approach to note-taking. Use different colors or symbols to graphically identify things like important concepts, vocabulary terms, queries, etc. Periodically review and compress notes while the knowledge is still fresh. Having effective organization not only helps you keep on top of obligations, it'll prevent late/missed assignments or appointments.

Goal-setting and Project Management

Working towards huge goals or complex tasks might feel daunting without planning and tracking procedures. Adopt goal-setting frameworks like SMART goals (specific, measurable, achievable, relevant, timebound) to design manageable milestones.

For initiatives, lay out step-by-step action plans recognizing prerequisites, resources needed, and interim deliverables. Leverage visual tools like Kanban boards or Gantt charts for planning out workflows across many workstreams. Time-tracking software can reveal where your efforts are being depleted.

Periodically assess your goals/projects and change as needed based on shifting priorities. Celebrate wins along the road!

Optimizing how you allocate your time, being organized, and pursuing your aspirations systematically provides a great edge for tackling heavier obligations down the line. Start nurturing these qualities now for lasting habits.

Problem-Solving and Teamwork

Regardless of what future vocation you select, you'll certainly experience barriers, challenges, and complex problems demanding creative answers. You'll also need to collaborate with others. Developing strong problem-solving talents paired with interpersonal team skills can equip you to conquer any challenge.

Problem-Solving Process
Rather than falling into frustration when faced with a challenging circumstance, follow a set

problem-solving procedure for working through it logically. First, gain clarity by clearly pinpointing the fundamental issue - using approaches like the "Five Whys" to peel apart surface-level symptoms. Then research to obtain all essential data and context surrounding the situation.

From there, generate many alternative solutions by ideating freely and investigating as many dissimilar options as feasible. Leverage creative thinking strategies like brainstorming, free-writing, mind-mapping, or even consulting various opinions. Evaluate the benefits, drawbacks, and feasibility of each offered option before selecting the strongest path ahead.

After implementing your action plan, reflect on the outcomes. If issues remain, return to studying root causes or iterating on the solution. Dissect what worked, what didn't, and lessons learned to develop your critical thinking abilities.

Throughout any problem-solving scenario, maintaining an open mindset is key. Avoid mental impediments like confirmation bias or functional fixedness that impede breakthroughs. Reframe obstacles as opportunities to flex your ingenuity. Nurturing a growth mindset willing to endure obstacles creates resilience.

Teamwork and Collaboration

While training autonomous problem-solving abilities is vital, many professional difficulties require coordinating team efforts across varied viewpoints, skill sets, and positions.

Emotional intelligence serves as the foundation for delivering constructive feedback, resolving disagreements, and finding compromise with people gracefully. Having empathy for team members' motivations and needs promotes interpersonal dynamics and trust.

Proactively communicating goals, roles, progress, and blockers transparently keeps bigger team activities connected and mitigates breakdowns. Looking out for opportunities to provide support to others, not merely deferring to self-interests, is anticipated.

Facilitate group problem-solving sessions by providing an inclusive environment where all ideas are embraced without judgment during initial brainstorming phases. As a facilitator, seek to draw out quieter voices and varied ideas before settling on joint decisions. Clarity regarding the next steps and accountabilities is crucial following any group meetings.

Don't wait for leadership roles to start exercising these skills. Seek team project chances through group assignments, extracurricular activities, community groups, or part-time work. You'll quickly notice how teamwork multiplies creative output and effect.

Developing your problem-solving expertise paired with the ability to work across teams creates a formidable future skillset for developing solutions and achieving significant change.

Chapter Six

Earning and Managing Money

Budgeting and Saving for Goals

Money management skills aren't taught nearly enough, yet understanding the foundations of budgeting and saving from an early age sets you up for lifelong financial wellness and reaching large goals. As a driven tween, take control by creating these key habits now:

Creating a Budget

The first step is identifying where your money currently goes each month. For income sources, this could include allowance, gift money, revenue from jobs/chores, etc. Categorize all expenses, no matter how tiny - consider refreshments, entertainment, clothing, and activity fees.

Once you can envision your cash inflows and outflows, you're ready to design an actual budget directing future money towards requirements (non-negotiable costs), wants (extras/fun), savings goals, and any other financial obligations. Budgeting tools and applications like Mint can help automate tracking.

It's vital to set a target for how much you want to save each month. Even putting away just 10% of earnings creates solid savings discipline. Watching your savings constantly build is tremendously encouraging for chasing bigger ambitions!

Curbing Spending Leaks

Of course, to save effectively, you also need spending awareness to eliminate excessive outlays. Temporary spending freezes or no-spend challenges provide valuable reality checks on your habits and pain areas surrounding avoiding needless expenditures.

Learn cost-saving tactics including meal planning, buying slightly used products, timing large purchases during sales, identifying wants vs needs before checkout, and exploring free/affordable entertainment opportunities in your neighborhood. Redirecting subscription services into savings is an easy victory.

Setting SMART Savings Goals

Having a particular goal in mind like saving for a new laptop, car, college tuition or first home helps sacrifices feel meaningful. Apply the SMART criteria to define a particular overall savings target, calculate measurable milestones, confirm it's realistically achievable within your resources/timeframe, maintain goals relevant to your present priorities, and attach a target timeline to achieve the finish line.

Celebrate financial accomplishments with little prizes to reinforce habit consistency. Sharing goals with money-minded people allows supporting each other. Modeling appropriate savings habits now ensures finance management becomes second nature when higher life costs arise.

Tween Entrepreneurship Ideas

Earning money doesn't have to mean waiting for an after-school job. There are great entrepreneurial prospects putting tween desire and creativity into action now. Not only can you start generational wealth-building early, but starting your own company promotes critical business knowledge and life skills:

Freelance Services

One of the easiest methods to monetize existing talents is by selling freelance services to neighbors, family friends, or your local community. Avenues could include tutoring younger children in academic areas, coaching sports/music classes, pet sitting/dog walking, tech support for setting up smart home gadgets, or freelance writing services. Market your knowledge using social media and neighborhood groups.

Product-Based Businesses

For the talented tween, setting up an internet shop or manning booths at local fairs enables selling created things for profit. Popular tween business ideas include handcrafted jewelry/accessories, baked goods, graphic design services like bespoke phone cases, calligraphy/hand-lettering, homemade bath products, candles, or repurposed furniture/home décor projects.

Reselling/Dropshipping

With relatively minimal startup expenses, tweens can buy discounted or freelanced things to resell at a markup using new or existing channels. Profitable niches could include sneaker resale, buying secondhand video games/books to resell online, putting up an eBay or Poshmark business to flip thrift clothing/accessories, or dropshipping products through sites like Etsy or Amazon FBA.

Blogging/Influencer Path

The entrepreneurial medium of today is utilizing the creator economy to contribute expertise, opinion, or lifestyle content. Tweens may monetize a YouTube channel, blog, Instagram, or TikTok following with brand sponsorships, affiliate money, and audience support through sites like Patreon once they acquire enough of a loyal following.

Whichever path you take, the entrepreneurial experience teaches financial literacy, strategic thinking, salesmanship, marketing, work ethic, and overcoming rejection. It encourages skills like tenacity, resourcefulness, learning to deliver value, offering outstanding customer service, and discovering creative solutions.

Introduction to Banking

You've tackled budgeting, saving objectives, and maybe bringing in an income source. But there's much more to learn about managing your money effectively through banking products and services meant to help finances grow over time. Understanding essential banking principles builds a firm foundation:

Bank Accounts

Piggy banks can only contain so much cash before it needs a secure place to accumulate. Opening a bank account establishes a safe repository for depositing, storing, and accessing money while also enabling transactions.

The two primary types of accounts are checking (used for regular banking and spending needs) and savings (designed for developing money over longer periods). Checking accounts assist in making purchases with debit cards or cash withdrawals, paying bills, depositing income, making transfers, etc. Savings accounts yield income but involve generally less freedom in accessing cash.

Compare fees, interest rates, minimums, ATM networks, and digital access while assessing account options at brick-and-mortar banks or online banking platforms. As a tween, you'll need an adult joint account holder, but maintaining a strong financial track record promotes independence access later.

Debit vs Credit Cards

Using debit cards deducts money directly from your checking account balance to pay for purchases. They provide the same purchasing power as credit cards but avoid creating debt since you're spending your dollars. Debit cards are useful for creating disciplined spending habits.

Credit cards let you borrow money from a line of credit to make purchases, then refund the amount later. utilized correctly, they assist build a credit history, provide fraud protection, earn incentives, and take advantage of interest-free grace periods. However, carrying huge sums and making late payments can lead to exorbitant interest costs and penalties that snowball debt.

Credit Scores

Speaking about credit, your credit score is a numeric rating derived from your borrowing and payback history that indicates how reliably you manage debt commitments. It's computed based on characteristics including payment history, quantities owing, credit mix, new accounts established, and duration of credit history.

Maintaining a good credit score by exercising responsible borrowing habits (consistently paying bills on time and keeping low credit utilization) qualifies you for loans with cheaper interest rates and fees. It also affects rental applications, insurance premiums, and even job possibilities by serving as a measure of overall financial responsibility.

Building Banking Relationships

Beyond money management tools, banks provide a range of other services - from loans to investing assistance and asset protection solutions that become more significant as you grow in life.

Developing a solid rapport with bankers allows them to understand your specific financial goals and provide customized advice/recommendations geared to your developing needs. Start creating banking relationships immediately with open communication and persistent positive behavior.

Chapter Seven

Work-Life Balance

Exploring Hobbies and Passions

While putting concentration on academics and future professional growth is admirable, make sure you don't neglect to explore things that kindle your passion and allow you to recharge. Engaging in hobbies and fostering personal passions aren't simply pleasurable activities — they're crucial channels for creativity, stress alleviation and even exposing latent skills.

Discovering Interests
If you're wondering what hobbies could enthrall you, start by looking inside at topics or activities you're naturally inclined to or dominated your interests as a child. Or explore for whole new

pursuits that inspire curiosity. Maybe it's painting, creative writing, coding, photography, gardening, music, chess, yoga, hiking or carpentry. The options are infinite!

Online resources and your local library/community centers are wonderful for exploring potential hobby possibilities and their benefits. Experiment with diverse domains until you unearth the ones that energize you. For exceptionally pricy hobbies with financial barriers to entry, explore innovative solutions like borrowing gear or recycling household items.

Developing Skills

As you engage yourself totally in hobbies, you begin developing new skills spontaneously. It's tremendously fulfilling having those "aha" moments of progress and capability milestones. These skills could include technical disciplines like coding languages or equipment expertise, artistic outlets like cinematography or graphics, or even transferable soft qualities like tenacity, attention, and problem-solving.

Embracing a "learn-it-all" approach helps continuously level up. Find manuals, teachers, workshops, or online lessons to boost your talents with training. Practice consistently and learn from mistakes without self-criticism. Create personal projects or join hobby communities to obtain additional hands-on experience and constructive feedback.

Monetizing Passions
Your hobbies may even turn into revenue streams or professional passions you're able to monetize as side employment, freelancing work, or future career ambitions. What starts as a basic passion in photography, fashion design, videography, blogging, jewelry-making, or music could blossom into creating a small business or service offering.

Being sincerely passionate about an issue naturally inspires the drive to become an expert and find unique methods to give value to potential clients or companies. With hard effort and determination, you might initiate a route to earning additional money while exploring entrepreneurial and career possibilities more thoroughly tied to your passions.

Above all, create time for hobbies and guilt-free de-stressing. Pursuing true passion projects increases life experience, stimulates imagination, and keeps you balanced despite other duties.

Managing Stress and Overwhelm

Let's face it, pursuing huge objectives and ambitions while balancing academics, extracurriculars, and personal obligations produces inherent difficulties. Left uncontrolled, stress evolves into burnout, emotional tiredness, and worsening mental health. That's why it's vital to establish coping methods for managing stress and avoiding becoming overwhelmed.

Identify Stressors

The first stage is determining your main triggers and sources of tension. Is it issues with procrastination, a continual sense of being rushed, tension with parents/siblings, social pressures, specific academic anxieties around test achievement, or general worry about the future? Getting granular about fundamental reasons provides targets for building tailored coping skills.

Physical Outlets

When feeling overworked, engaging your body through exercise, yoga, martial arts or even simply a quick walk around the neighborhood gives enormous stress relief by releasing pent-up tensions and stimulating blood flow. The endorphins from physical activity increase your happiness, confidence, and concentration.

Mindfulness Practices

Science reveals methods like controlled breathing, meditation, gradual muscular relaxation, and guided visualization boost your ability to remain calm and quiet racing thoughts among chaos. Start by committing simply 5-10 minutes per day to mindfulness activities. Over time, you'll improve distress tolerance and gain greater emotional regulation during stressful circumstances.

Journaling and Reflection

Getting spinning worries out of your head and onto paper (or a digital document) allows you to start processing stressors more objectively versus letting your thoughts continue cycling through anxious loops. Journaling is an expressive tool for defusing overpowering emotions and staying grounded.

Other useful strategies include listening to relaxing music, leaning into your support system by opening up to trustworthy friends/mentors, and consciously scheduling guilt-free downtime for partaking in preferred activities or just mentally recharging. Getting proper sleep, diet, and hydration is crucial too.

By being proactive about handling stresses now, you create resilience for withstanding future demands. Having coping methods gives reassuring safety nets to avoid crumbling through unavoidable obstacles life delivers.

Importance of Family and Friends

As you actively work towards your career aspirations and personal improvement, never underestimate the vital importance your closest relationships play in bolstering your tenacity, self-belief, and general well-being. Strong family and friend support systems encourage failures, celebrate your accomplishments, and remind you of what's most meaningful.

Family Bonds

For all their foibles, your parents, siblings, and extended family have created your basic personality and imprinted formative beliefs. Even amid disputes or conflicting opinions, keeping communication lines open fosters trustworthy ties and sources of unconditional love throughout challenging times.

Your family understands you in really intimate ways - talents, motivators, insecurities, and all. They can offer specific insight and belief in your potential that promotes decision-making, goal-setting, and resiliency. Be intentional about expressing thanks and checking in with family members. Emotional support increases stability.

Friend Circles

As you progress into your tween years, platonic friendships become crucial supportive interactions beyond the family nucleus. Positive buddy groups provide channels for relating through common interests and life experiences. There's a special comfort in exploring identity alongside people undergoing similar key transformations.

Surrounding oneself with motivated, inspiring individuals who share your desire and goal acts as reciprocal inspiration for bettering each other. You can share advice, cooperate on projects, and keep each other grounded during inevitable ups and downs on your journeys. Embrace differences too — diversity among friends expands viewpoints.

Being part of a strong community brings empowerment and accountability for personal improvement. Put away uncertainty and competitiveness – truly praising each other's triumphs, not comparison, is what nourishes true friendships.

Overall Well-Being

Ultimately, developing your fundamental relationships and allowing yourself to experience life's joys alongside loved ones contributes immensely to your total fulfillment, happiness, and feeling of purpose beyond just work honors.

Make attempts to be fully present during quality time instead of burying your head in work. Little traditions like game evenings, weekend getaways, or creative endeavors with friends/family produce cherished memories, inside jokes, and anecdotes that connect you. These are the moments that persist through difficult circumstances.

Balance professional ambitions with safeguarding your emotional energy, so you have enough to invest in the relationships that keep you grounded. For overall well-being, tend to both objectives and connections intentionally. Those helpful folks are what give meaning to achievement.

Chapter Eight

Getting Experience

Volunteering Opportunities

One of the most satisfying ways to get vital real-world experience and build critical skills is through volunteering your time and talents. Don't overlook the great importance of community work beyond only earning credit or awards. Thoughtfully selected volunteering exposes you to varied environments, networking chances, and direct insight into potential career pathways.

Identifying Causes/Organizations

The first stage is finding causes, topics, or organizations you feel passionate about supporting.

Animal welfare? Environmental activism? Youth mentorship? Medical/hospital volunteering? Local community service projects? When you have a genuine personal connection to the mission, your involvement and potential for impact expand.

Consider your existing capabilities, hobbies, and logistical factors like transportation abilities or scheduling flexibility. Explore VolunteerMatch and JustServe to search volunteer openings by location and cause area. Your school's community service coordinator likely maintains a list of partner groups too.

Camping youth summer camps or afterschool programs could appeal if you appreciate interacting with children and growing mentorship skills. For aspiring teachers or coaches, NGOs like Boys & Girls Clubs provide opportunities to lead enrichment activities.

Hospital and healthcare facility volunteers connect directly with patients and staff, providing invaluable insight into medicine, patient care, and day-to-day hospital operations. Outdoor enthusiasts may gravitate toward national park service possibilities or local environmental conservancy activities.

Transferable Skill Development

No matter which cause or group resonates, volunteering provides universally transferable abilities for any future vocation. Customer service experience comes from connecting with community members. Event planning and logistical coordination build project management ability. Public speaking and leadership occur when facilitating group activities.

The emotional intelligence obtained through community contacts is vital too - traits like empathy, cultural awareness, clear communication, and conflict resolution are all enhanced while working with various groups. You acquire experience cooperating across teams and addressing real-world difficulties through volunteering.

College Applications and Resumes

Beyond personal growth, volunteering enables you to construct convincing narratives around your experiences for future college entrance essays and job applications. Admissions officers and hiring managers appreciate individuals who've sustained long-term volunteering commitments and can communicate insights regarding the skills developed, problems faced, and overall takeaways.

Quantifying your community impact through metrics like hours served, individuals aided, monies raised, or programming implemented allows you to demonstrate tangible value creation. Avenues for development into enhanced duties, specialized jobs, or young committees/boards indicate leadership ability.

Getting started with volunteering throughout the tween years offers you an early professional perspective for being accountable, displaying initiative, and earning confidence via practical experience in dynamic circumstances. These vital lessons prepare you for even deeper experiential learning through work shadowing and career exploration programs.

Job Shadowing a Professional

While investigating new career sectors through research, media, and conversations is instructive, there's no matching the revelatory experience of observing professionals in action directly through job shadowing. This immersion approach allows you to evaluate day-to-day realities, duties, and working cultures before committing further along courses.

Arranging Job Shadows

The first stage is determining which vocations best tickle your interest and connect with your inherent talents or emerging skill sets. Careers to consider could originate from your favorite class subjects like healthcare roles for scientific fans or computer programming for the tech-savvy.

Next, tap into your network of familial or community ties to see if any relatives, family friends, parents of students, or neighbors have positions you could shadow. When submitting inquiries, offer an overview of your background and willingness to learn about your role. Propose booking a few hours or perhaps a whole day for your visit.

Shadowing Etiquette

Once shadowing has been arranged, prepare thoughtful questions regarding usual tasks, paths for entering the sector, work conditions, growth prospects, and work/life balance. Request a tour of the workplace to acquire visibility into the atmospherics and prospective colleague relationships.

Dress professionally in business casual attire to give a polished first impression. Carry a notepad for writing down observations throughout the experience — tiny nuances often expose fascinating viewpoints regarding the day-to-day demands and business culture fit.

During downtime, ask your host about their work journey, professional triumphs, and struggles, or what they wish they knew before selecting the post. These personal experiences convey authenticity beyond only the technical work duties.

Follow Up Reflections
Within 48 hours following your shadowing experience, send a handwritten thank you note expressing appreciation for the person's kind time

and mentorship. This sophisticated gesture indicates your maturity and curiosity.

Then, look back on everything you observed for insights aligning with or conflicting with your initial expectations about the role. Use this greater clarity to either validate continuing pursuit of the career route or shift your exploration elsewhere based on first-hand reality.

The significant knowledge received through work shadowing fast-tracks your career discovery path by basing your perspective on observable truths rather than just theoretical assumptions.

Attending Career Fairs and Events

While individual job shadowing provides an intimate insight into specific professions, career fairs, and exploration events offer unprecedented possibilities to cast a wider net across numerous fields, organizations, and industries concurrently. These educational experiences link you directly with working professionals sharing insight and advice.

Preparing to Attend

Research which companies, colleges, and organizations will have exhibitor booths by reading the event's registration details. Note any panels, workshops, or speakers catching your eye for sessions providing frameworks on the career search process, entrepreneurship, college planning, or advice within specialized industries.

Prepare copies of your professional resume displaying relevant experience, talents, and academic achievements so far. Have an elevator pitch outlining your history and primary aims for attending the event — this shows clear intent when initiating talks.

Most importantly, brainstorm intelligent questions you'd want to ask leaders from your industries of interest. Going in with deliberate queries displays excitement and an actively inquisitive mentality vs appearing uninterested.

Working the Room

With research in hand, organize your time effectively between sessions and visiting exhibitors. Dress professionally in business casual clothing. Approach exhibitor booths during downtime between your main events to avoid being unpleasant.

Introduce yourself with a confident handshake and your elevator pitch to initiate rapport. Quickly transition into your inquiries about work settings, mobility upwards, obstacles versus rewards, desirable backgrounds and talents for recruiting, and any sagacious advice for eager kids investigating their professional pathways. Representatives value intellectual curiosity.

Collect contact information or business cards from folks you are particularly connected with. Be sure to bring a notepad for noting significant points and prospective next steps like following up on internship programs, site visit opportunities, or informational interviews.

Post-Event Recap

Within 24 hours following the career event, send courteous follow-up emails to any contacts made reaffirming your thanks for their input. Summarize important findings, lessons learned, and how you plan to activate future steps from their direction.

Then frequently examine all your notes from sessions and exhibitor talks, synthesizing broad themes or new ways you may wish to swing your career exploration trajectory. Having fresh professional wisdom and myth-busting about particular approaches improves your clarity.

Events provide an unrivaled chance to develop new contacts while being exposed to varied ideas beyond simply your initial research. By proactively attending and immersing oneself, you display ambition in taking responsibility for your future.

Chapter Nine

Believing in Yourself

Building Confidence

Confidence is that unwavering self-assurance that propels you through problems and allows your unique talents to show. A confident mindset isn't about arrogance or bluster – true confidence derives from self-awareness, valuing your worth, and knowing you can manage anything life delivers. Developing unshakable confidence as a tween provides the groundwork for resiliency through life's ups and downs.

Recognize Your Strengths
One of the biggest culprits eroding confidence is fixating on perceived inadequacies or problem areas instead of embracing your stellar qualities. Start

redirecting that inner dialogue by compiling a list of all the positive characteristics, abilities, talents, and accomplishments that make you exceptional. This could include attributes like creativity, determination, empathy, or intellectual abilities.

Next, allow those who care about you to add their thoughts on your powers to round out a full vision of what makes you shine. Identify personal "wins" or successes — from earned rewards to obstacles you've already defeated via determination. Celebrating triumphs increases confidence.

Practice Self-Appreciation

In addition to discovering your talents, you need to actively practice appreciating yourself through positive self-talk and shutting down harsh inner critics. Catch and reframe negative thoughts like "I'm so bad at public speaking" to "I get nervous sometimes, but I'm working on improving my skills."

Monitor for people in your life transmitting insecurities onto you through backhanded "compliments" that make you doubt yourself. Setting boundaries around negativity in your settings preserves self-worth.

Find Power in Vulnerability

Counterintuitively, being vulnerable enough to admit worries, blunders or fears takes enormous inner confidence and fortitude. Those who can own their challenges or inadequacies with humility and a drive to learn and better come across as remarkably self-assured.

Embrace imperfection as part of the journey instead of attaching your self-worth to obtaining perfection. Asking for help, direction or clarification isn't a weakness — it's self-awareness boosting your growth.

Your Personal Brand

How you show up and exhibit confidence affects how others perceive your credibility, composure, and influence. Work on building a great personal brand through your spoken and physical communication style and presence.

Practice creating direct eye contact in conversations and sporting an upright stance that communicates openness, involvement, and active listening. Monitor filler phrases like "um" that might weaken authority. Grooming, hygiene, and how you hold yourself visually also impact perceptions. Envisioning achievement fuels self-assured body language.

Building true confidence is an iterative process of overcoming concerns, embracing your unique brilliance, and staying grounded during upheaval. Have faith in developing your talents via continual study, and conviction that you can accomplish everything you wish.

Overcoming Fears and Doubts

Even with rising confidence, chasing big goals ensures facing periods of self-doubt, fears, and emotional stumbling blocks along the path. Thoughts like "What if I'm not good enough?" or catastrophizing about worst-case scenarios are hurdles taking a tremendous mental toll.

Identifying Your Fears and Doubt Patterns

To disarm concerns and doubts, you first need to bring them out into the open by explicitly expressing your apprehensions. Is it fear of failure, rejection, ridicule, or the unknown that bothers you most often? Are there some settings like public speaking or testing environments that elicit overwhelming uneasiness and negativity?

Next, bring self-awareness to your regular routines around concern and avoidance. Do you postpone taking risks? Catastrophize events into more dramatic fiction than reality? Making excuses or people-pleasing instead of asserting yourself? Those programmed reflexes reinforce worries taking hold.

Reframing Limiting Beliefs

To remove fears' grasp, you must actively face and redefine the limiting beliefs and narratives pushing those anxieties. Challenge unreasonable notions blocking you from pursuing aspirations due to "What if?" anxieties. Replace those thinking loops with empowered, solution-focused concerns like "How can I best prepare?" or "What resources are available to help me succeed?"

Creating coping mechanism action plans for working through concerns during specific scenarios renders them less scary. For example, build pre-presentation routines involving breathing exercises, power postures, positive mantras, and rigorous preparation if public speaking produces panic.

Visualizing Desired Outcomes

One of the most potent confidence-builders is imagining yourself already successful and taking intentional measures towards those results. See yourself poised, capable, and oozing assuredness as you take risks, rise above problems, and defy nagging doubts.

Frequently engage in that vision through guided visualization exercises or mentally scripting desirable scenarios before key events - like acceptances, nailing interviews, award recognition moments, or delivering compelling speeches. Your subconscious will start embracing the self-image you reinforce.

The more you practice staring down anxieties through realistic preparation, reframing negativity into empowerment, and forcing yourself ahead, the smaller those doubt-based challenges become. Anxiety diminishes when you accumulate reference experiences overcoming your constraints.

Finding Role Models and Mentors

Pursuing your passion-fueled ambitions is an amazing yet overwhelming path at times. That's why it's vital to have exemplars lighting the route — role models who inspire you and mentors delivering specific instruction as motivating factors.

The Power of Role Models

Think of role models as the personification of where you aim to go and who you aspire to become one day through pure devotion and focus. They exemplify what's possible by conquering identical hurdles and roadblocks you're facing now.

Identifying role models could involve investigating the lives and ideas of public personalities, industry leaders, or visionaries you like for their grit, talents, and impact. However, role models can be found closer to home too through observing instructors, family friends, or local community members whose values, perseverance, and ideals set them apart.

There's no need to directly know these persons for them to inspire your motivation. Creating vision boards with images, phrases and crucial biographical facts about role models boosts their power. Picture their power in instances when you need perspective or boosts of encouragement through challenging stretches.

Finding Mentors

While role models are inspirations from afar, mentors occupy a more personalized role of wisdom sharers directly guiding your personal and professional development through continuous encounters. Carefully choose potential mentors based on characteristics like their experience, areas of knowledge you're growing in, or personal traits/philosophies that resonate profoundly with you.

School workers, family members, local business owners, and community groups are wonderful areas to find mentorship relationships. Briefly identify yourself and describe why you like the person, then query about their willingness to a mentorship relationship either in person or digitally.

Come prepared with insightful questions for each mentoring session ranging from guidance on issues you're encountering, insight around growing specific abilities, best practices for networking and promoting yourself, their tales of lessons gained, and responsibility around goals. Then listen with a receptive mindset and apply their expertise sincerely.

Foster the relationship by updating mentors on your progress, honoring their time investment through occasional gestures of thanks, and respecting any boundaries they've set. Building rapport and trust uncovers deeper wells of insight customized particularly to your enrichment.

Having a network of role models exemplifying inspirational paths paired with mentors' specific directions speeds up your progress significantly. You'll discover lessons generally reserved through years of hard-won experience, giving you a jump start on success!

Chapter Ten

Involving Family

Having Career Conversations

While building your way towards satisfying objectives is liberating, your parents and close family members can be helpful allies in your job exploration journey — if you initiate open and fruitful interactions. They give viewpoints informed by their life experiences, wisdom, and genuine wants for you to grow.

Creating Safe Spaces for Dialogue

The first step is establishing a safe, judgment-free environment where everyone feels comfortable voicing thoughts, concerns, or advice without fear of conflict or dismissal. Clearly explain your hopes for mutual respect and objectivity during these sessions.

You may need to refute any preconceived assumptions your parents have about specific career options you're contemplating based on societal influences or their backgrounds. Invite them to approach with curiosity vs assumptions about your motivations.

If family connections have historically been strained around challenging conversations, consider heading to a neutral area free of distractions and ornery siblings. Or enlist a third-party mediator who can sustain productive communication.

Sharing Your Passions

Once you've created the right tone, take the lead by presenting your latest career exploration activities, interests, or findings with enthusiasm. Describe what drives you to particular sectors and how your talents fit with prospective opportunities you've identified.

Avoid anyTemRecensiot your parents placed preconceived biases onto you regarding prestigious occupations. This is about you illuminating your true drivers directly from the heart. Their responsibility is to listen attentively with an open mind.

Solicit Their Perspectives

After you've explained your thought process, encourage your parents to react by giving any ideas from their life experiences that could expand your viewpoints. Perhaps components of their careers exposed them to positive or bad features you've not considered.

Encourage them to voice any specific concerns they may have too - whether practical factors like earning potential, work/life harmony, or ethical reservations about particular businesses. Having these candid chats productively addresses worries.

If your family's cultural heritage or religious systems influence their viewpoints greatly, ask them to expand on those circumstances so you may grasp their stances more thoroughly.

The key is sustaining a reciprocal flow of healthy communication where everyone is heard, experiences are shared objectively and knowledge gets imparted – not dictated – with your development's best interests as the common aim.

Setting Expectations with Parents

During your open career chats, it's helpful to connect on certain realistic expectations and boundaries upfront with your parents for this collaborative inquiry. A few crucial areas to solidify include:

Financial Considerations

Depending on your family's financial circumstances, there may need to be transparency around budgets, responsibilities for funding different career development routes, and general fiscal restrictions.

Perhaps your parents are willing to pay for some enrichment activities, job shadowing opportunities, skills training, or higher education aspirations if you exhibit consistent devotion. Or there may be an expectation for you to earn and contribute financially to your professional investments.

Either way, having an upfront grasp of what monetary resources exist – and which expenses fall under your responsibility – allows you to prepare and make informed decisions accordingly without unrealistic assumptions.

Time Commitments

Similarly, consider realistic time commitments and calendar management to ensure personal obligations don't become unduly onerous. If investing in extracurricular leadership roles, part-time work, volunteering, or entrepreneurial efforts, be open about involvement levels.

Your parents may require reassurance that your career goals won't come at the price of familial responsibilities, self-care, and work/life balance. Proactively acknowledging priorities fosters responsibility.

Decision Roles & Veto Powers

As your career exploration advances, certain milestones like picking probable college majors or narrowing career options will include critical decisions. Determine beforehand what amount of input, veto powers, or ultimate decision authority your parents intend to have in those choices based on legal parameters, financial dependencies, or personal opinions.

If asserting your independence to make autonomous choices is crucial, that position should be explicitly articulated and appreciated as well. While advice and recommendations are helpful, unrestrained veto powers could engender resentment.

The goal is to create mutually agreed-upon expectations for everyone's responsibilities, duties, and boundaries from the outset. This upfront agreement promotes credibility and positive rapport as you advance together on this trip.

Making a Career Plan Together

With meaningful conversations facilitating transparency and mutual respect, you can now harness the power of family engagement by cooperatively constructing a thorough professional action plan including all the insights offered.

Assess Your Current Situation

Begin by taking stock of your current circumstances across academics, finances, time commitments, and any other priorities or limits. This clear-eyed picture of your circumstances along with self-evaluations around basic beliefs, interests, and skill strengths create the direction.

Identify Your Motivating Goals

Then, get laser-focused by vividly describing your overarching professional goals and the reasons those aims resonate so powerfully. Attaching impassioned context around your "whys" preserves everyone's inspiration through approaching milepost preparation.

Map Out Exploratory Activities

With big-picture objectives identified, build out a path for acquiring additional hands-on experience across key topics of interest. Include action plans for job shadowing, volunteering, training programs, internships, or entrepreneurial enterprises to start piloting. Your parents may have connections opening doors.

Discuss internalized ideas like embedding skill-building habits into everyday routines like reading periodicals, taking online classes, or practicing public speaking regularly. Incremental action drives progress.

Brainstorm Backup Scenarios
No plan survives an encounter with reality unmodified. So together theorize future impediments or backup scenarios necessitating alternative paths. From moving industries owing to eye-opening realizations to managing failures or setbacks via resilience – having moldable contingencies sustains forward mobility.

Outline Advisor Roles and Resources

Finalize who fills essential adviser responsibilities for teaching you through diverse scenarios and offering resources or support across academics, professional skills, financial aid, networking, interviews, and significant decision points.

While parents may oversee components closest to family life, identify community people, teachers, mentors or professionals fit for additional advisor positions. Identify limits and communication methods.

Your proactive involvement of parental advice, wisdom, and accountability in building this action plan demonstrates maturity while improving family teamwork. With everyone aligned, you become an unstoppable force actualizing your grand visions!

30 emerging career that will shape the future job market

The future work market is continually evolving, driven by technical developments, global trends, and societal upheavals. As we progress toward a more digitized and sustainable society, new vocations are emerging to match the shifting demands. Here are 30 developing vocations that are expected to affect the future labor market:

1. Artificial Intelligence (AI) Specialist: With the increasing rise of AI and machine learning, specialists who can create, train, and optimize AI systems will be in great demand across numerous industries.

2. Cybersecurity Expert: As cyber threats continue to rise, the demand for cybersecurity specialists who can secure digital assets and minimize risks will remain critical.

3. Virtual Reality (VR) Developer: The uses of VR are extending beyond gaming into industries like healthcare, education, and real estate, offering opportunities for VR developers.

4. Drone Pilot/Operator: The use of drones is rising in areas such as agriculture, construction, delivery services, and public safety, needing professional drone operators.

5. Sustainable Energy Specialist: With the increased emphasis on renewable energy sources, professionals in wind, solar, and other green technologies will be vital for transitioning to a sustainable future.

6. Data Scientist: The capacity to extract insights from enormous amounts of data will continue to be beneficial across sectors, creating the need for data scientists.

7. Genetic Counselor: As personalized medicine and genetic testing grow more popular, genetic counselors will play a critical role in interpreting genetic information and guiding patients.

8. Robotics Engineer: The integration of robotics in manufacturing, healthcare, and other industries will offer possibilities for engineers who can design, develop, and maintain robotic systems.

9. 3D Printing Specialist: With the increasing usage of 3D printing in numerous industries, professionals who can design, operate, and repair 3D printers will be in high demand.

10. Blockchain Developer: As blockchain technology continues to disrupt industries like finance, supply chain, and healthcare, talented blockchain developers will be needed.

11. Urban Farmer/Vertical Farming Technician: With the growing need for sustainable food production in urban settings, urban farming and vertical farming technicians will play a critical role.

12. Telemedicine Physician/Nurse: The rise of telemedicine and remote healthcare services will generate opportunities for physicians and nurses who can provide virtual consultations and care.

13. Social Media Manager: As organizations continue to embrace social media for marketing and consumer involvement, social media managers who can establish and execute effective plans will be sought.

14. Augmented Reality (AR) Developer: AR applications are spreading into domains including retail, gaming, and education, offering opportunities for developers specializing in AR technology.

15. Nanotechnology Engineer: The development and application of nanotechnology in fields like medical, electronics, and materials science will fuel the need for nanotechnology engineers.

16. Sustainability Consultant: Organizations across industries will require sustainability consultants to help them reduce their environmental effects and meet sustainability goals.

17. Esports Coach/Manager: With the advent of competitive gaming and esports, coaches and managers who can advise and support professional esports teams and players will be in demand.

18. Renewable Energy Vehicle Technician: As electric and alternative fuel vehicles grow more widespread, technicians proficient in maintaining and repairing these vehicles will be required.

19. Digital Wellness Counselor: With the increased reliance on technology and its possible impact on mental health, digital wellness counselors will assist individuals in maintaining a healthy relationship with technology.

20. Biomedical Engineer: The integration of engineering concepts with medical and biological sciences will generate opportunities for biomedical engineers in fields including prostheses, implants, and medical devices.

21. User Experience (UX) Designer: As businesses attempt to create seamless and intuitive digital experiences, the demand for UX designers who can optimize user interactions will continue to grow.

22. Cloud Computing Specialist: With the increasing popularity of cloud computing solutions, specialists who can design, develop, and maintain cloud infrastructure will be increasingly sought after.

23. Cryptography Expert: As data security becomes vital, professionals in cryptography who can develop and apply advanced encryption techniques will be crucial.

24. Virtual Assistant Developer: The rise of virtual assistants and conversational AI will require developers experienced in natural language processing and conversational interface design.

25. Geospatial Data Analyst: The usage of geospatial data in sectors like urban planning, environmental monitoring, and logistics will boost the need for analysts who can understand and analyze spatial data.

26. Robotics Technician: As robots grow increasingly prominent in manufacturing, healthcare, and other industries, technicians who can maintain, repair, and program these robots will be in high demand.

27. Bioinformatics Scientist: The convergence of computer science and biology will offer opportunities for bioinformatics scientists who can analyze and understand complicated biological data.

28. Recycling Coordinator: With the increased emphasis on waste management and circular economies, recycling coordinators will play a critical role in planning and implementing successful recycling plans.

29. Autonomous Vehicle Engineer: As self-driving automobiles and autonomous vehicles become a reality, engineers specializing in autonomous systems and vehicle automation will be important.

30. Climate Change Analyst: With the increased focus on mitigating and adapting to climate change, analysts who can model and evaluate climate data will be important in generating sustainable solutions.

These growing vocations represent just a glimpse into the future employment market, which will likely continue to expand as new technologies, problems, and opportunities arise. Embracing lifelong learning, adaptability, and readiness to upskill or reskill will be vital for individuals and companies to thrive in this quickly changing market.

Made in United States
Orlando, FL
21 April 2025